The World's Greatest Composers

Wolfgang Amadeus Mozart

by Michael White

OTHER TITLES IN THE SERIES
Ludwig van Beethoven by Pam Brown (1-85015-302-7)
John Lennon by Michael White (1-85015-304-3)
Peter Ilych Tchaikovsky by Michael Pollard (1-85015-303-5)
Antonio Vivaldi by Pam Brown (1-85015-301-9)
Coming Soon
Johann Sebastian Bach by Christopher Gibb (1-85015-311-6)
Frederic Chopin (1-85015-310-8)
Bob Marley (1-85015-312-4)

Picture Credits:
AGK: 5, 6 (top), 8, 9, 10, 11, 12-3, 12 (below), 16, 17, 30 (both), 38, 39, 40 (both), 41, 44-5, 46, 50, 51 (top left, below), 55; Art Resource: 4, 16; Catherine Ashmore: 48 (below), 54; e.t. archive: 59 (below); Mary Evans Picture Library: 14, 42, 45 (right), 47; Hulton-Deutsch Collection : 21, 24 (both), 56; Image Bank: 6, 58; Kobal Collection: 34, 51 (top right); Phillips Classical: 59 (top); Scala: 18-9, 26; Spectrum Colour Library: 33; Frank Spooner: 48 (top).

Published in Great Britain in 1992
by Exley Publications Ltd,
16 Chalk Hill, Watford,
Herts WD1 4BN, United Kingdom.

A copy of the CIP data is available from
the British Library on request

ISBN 1-85015-300-0

Series editor: Helen Exley
Editor: Samantha Armstrong
Picture editor: Alex Goldberg of Image Select
Typeset by Brush Off Studios, St Albans.
Printed by Cambus Litho Ltd, East Kilbride.

Wolfgang Amadeus
MOZART

Michael White

Acclaim in Bohemia

The last notes of music tumble away into the air and the audience bursts into tumultuous applause. The people continue to clap and whistle, roar with delight and shout for "more" for at least five minutes. Finally, a little man wearing a bright jacket and pure white wig, smiling broadly, walks through the crowd and approaches the orchestra in front of the stage. He turns to the audience, bows low, sweeping his arms in a loop before him, and seats himself at the pianoforte.

Silence falls over the audience, not a sound can be heard as the young man's hands are raised above the keyboard. Then, for the next half an hour he plays what one journalist at the time described as music unsurpassed by any other performer of the instrument. The audience is enthralled. At the end of the improvisation, the people rise to their feet again and the sound of their reception rings out in praise.

Again the little man returns to the pianoforte and entertains the audience with themes from his opera, *The Marriage of Figaro,* which he had composed the previous year. Then he plays intricate variations and cunningly-disguised melodies and harmonies from his other famous pieces.

The year is 1787. The place, Prague in a country then known as Bohemia. The musician, Wolfgang Amadeus Mozart.

This performance in January 1787 was probably the high point of Mozart's public success during his lifetime. Sadly, he never enjoyed this sort of reception in Vienna where he spent most of his adult life. The Viennese failed to appreciate his enormous

Opposite: Wolfgang Amadeus Mozart at about the time of his successful concerts in Prague, 1787. Throughout his short life Mozart's genius was heralded and then, just as quickly, ignored. Today, however, he is rightfully recognized as one of the greatest composers in the world.

Below: Mozart's apartment in Vienna. He lived on the second floor of this building.

Above: Today, in celebration of Mozart's genius, a whole industry has been built around his story. He is so popular that even boxes of chocolate with his portrait on the lid are sold, along with framed pictures, toffees and truffles. Salzburg and Vienna, making the most of their links with the composer, have "Mozartiana" everywhere. Ironically, they did not appreciate him during his lifetime.

talent, and he was frequently passed over for far lesser composers.

Mozart's true worth was only fully realized long after his death. Today, records, tapes and compact discs of his music sell in their millions throughout the world. His is probably the most popular classical music played in all five continents, and rivals sales of rock music such as that of the Beatles and Madonna.

In 1991, the bicentenary of Mozart's death, his entire works were released in a set comprising 180 compact discs. The collection takes over two hundred hours to listen to. Ironically, while many other composers of the time earned respectable salaries and enjoyed comfortable lives, during his short lifetime, Wolfgang Amadeus Mozart could never earn enough money to properly look after his family. Within five short, but amazingly creative, years of that great night in Prague, the world's greatest composer would die in debt, and be buried in an unmarked pauper's grave.

The age of revolution

Wolfgang Amadeus Mozart was born to Leopold and Anna Maria Mozart in the city of Salzburg, Austria on January 27, 1756.

Salzburg nestles in a valley at the northern edge of the Austrian Alps. In 1756, it was part of the Holy Roman Empire, presided over by Empress Maria Theresa and Emperor Francis I.

The Seven Years War began in the year of Mozart's birth and ended in a weakening of the Empire and a shift in the balance of power in Europe. At this time the power of the monarchy still held sway in many European countries, but this era was fading fast and revolution was not far away.

Over one hundred years before Mozart's birth, the English Civil War of 1642 had set the pattern for a form of democracy envied by many progressive thinkers in Europe.

It was also a time of great change in other spheres of life. In the world of science, the eighteenth century was the time known as the "Age of Enlightenment" when scientists made great strides in understanding the world.

Important writers and thinkers of the time included Voltaire, Jean-Jacques Rousseau and Montesquieu. Their revolutionary ideas about the rights of men and women and the freedom of the individual were to further the march to revolution by the end of the century.

Such change was also reflected in the music of the time. Throughout Europe, every cultured person wanted new, "modern" music, and musical styles were developing just as fast as politics, science and philosophy.

Mozart was born into an era rich in music. The great composers of the time included George Frederick Handel, Joseph Haydn and Christoph Gluck. But, within a few decades, all of these luminaries of music would be eclipsed by perhaps the greatest composer in history, by what one commentator described as "a Godlike genius", the little man from Salzburg, Wolfgang Amadeus Mozart.

"Mozart makes you believe in God – much more than going to church – because it cannot be by chance that such a phenomenon arrives into this world and then passes after thirty-six years, leaving behind such an unbounded number of unparalleled masterpieces."
Sir Georg Solti.

"In my dreams of Heaven, I always see the great Masters gathered in a huge hall in which they all reside. Only Mozart has his own suite."
Victor Borge.

A musical background

Wolfgang Mozart was especially small when he was born and developed into a thin and short child; in later life he never grew much beyond five feet tall.

Although he was cheerful and energetic, he was plagued by illness throughout his life. This was probably to do with the lack of hygiene and ignorance of medicine to which all levels of society were then susceptible.

Wolfgang was the seventh child of Leopold and Anna Maria but only the second to survive because of the high number of infant deaths.

Wolfgang's father was a well-educated, cultured man. He was a prominent musician and held the post of official composer to the Court of Salzburg. Leopold Mozart was also the author of a popular music book called *The Violin Method* that was used by most young musicians.

In the 1750s, Central Europe was divided into

Above: Getreidegasse in Salzburg where the Mozart family lived and where Wolfgang was born in 1754.

Right: The interior of the house in which the Mozarts lived from 1747 to 1773. Now a museum, the clavichord on which five-year-old Mozart learned to play and on which he composed his first pieces is still there, along with the violin which Leopold taught his young genius to play.

small city states governed by Princes or Electors who maintained lavish courts. The status of musicians in these states depended on the attitude of the ruler. Leopold Mozart was fortunate in that the ruler of Salzburg was interested in music and financed an orchestra presided over by a *Kapellmeister* (Master of the Chapel).

Leopold had the position of Vice-*Kapellmeister.* He did not earn a large salary because musicians were considered to have a social position little above that of a servant and were treated just like domestic staff. However, the Mozart home was always full of music and many fine instruments.

There were violins and recorders, a harpsichord and a clavichord in the house. Clavichords look like small pianos, but they have a more limited range and a softer tone than the pianos we know today.

The difference between a clavichord and a harpsichord is that the strings inside the clavichord are struck by hammers, much like the modern

Wolfgang's father, Leopold Mozart, in 1765. Leopold dominated Wolfgang's life in every way – Wolfgang did not even have any formal schooling apart from the lessons his father gave him. Determined to see his son succeed as a great musician and composer, Leopold pushed him relentlessly from a very early age.

piano, but the strings in a harpsichord are plucked by a device inside the instrument.

At the time of Mozart's birth the newly-invented forte-piano, or the pianoforte as it later became known, was a relatively rare and costly instrument, but a musician who had been taught to play the clavichord could learn the pianoforte fairly easily. The instrument got its name because, unlike its predecessors, it was able to produce both soft (piano), and loud (forte) sounds.

It was in this highly creative musical atmosphere that Wolfgang and his elder sister by five years, known as Nannerl, spent their childhood. It was their father, Leopold Mozart, who taught Wolfgang and his sister how to play a variety of instruments from home and it was also he who pushed them into becoming professional musicians at a very early age.

A musical prodigy

Wolfgang took a natural delight in most things. He was lively, bright and affectionate and enjoyed making up games with Nannerl. From an early age, he had a highly-developed sense of fun and was forever devising pranks to play on his family. He was messy and disorganized. He adored his parents and was extremely respectful and obedient, but despite the closeness of the family, he needed constant reassurances of affection.

In appearance, he was short and thin with a round, pale face and a shock of fair hair. Nannerl was considered a beauty by the age of eight or nine, and Wolfgang's parents had been known as the "handsomest couple in Salzburg". Wolfgang was not particularly good-looking, but, what he lacked in looks he made up for by sheer liveliness of character.

Nannerl was taught at home with daily music lessons as well as mathematics and writing. When Wolfgang was four, he began to interrupt his sister's music lessons. Ever since he was old enough to sit at a clavichord or to hold a child's violin he had been amusing himself by playing simple chords and scales. But, it was only when his father began to take notice and to include him in formal lessons with Nannerl that he began to realize the great natural talent his son possessed.

There are a wealth of stories from Wolfgang's childhood that chronicle the amazing musical feats he performed from a very early age.

Leopold quickly discovered that Wolfgang had perfect pitch. That is, he could tell if any note he heard was in tune with the standard or absolute range of notes. He could sing any note perfectly in tune and identify any note played to him. By the age of four, he could learn an entire minuet on the clavichord within half an hour.

One story tells how, at the age of four or five, he attempted to write a lengthy and ambitious concerto. Unknown to his father, Wolfgang had sat in the music room for several afternoons between lessons writing out a piece of music. One evening when the family was entertaining a musician friend of Leopold's, Wolfgang handed his father the manuscript he had been working on. At first glance, it looked nothing more than a jumble of meaningless notes, smudged with ink and written with an unsteady hand.

Leopold and his friend had smiled kindly at the boy's efforts. But, as they looked more closely they saw that the manuscript was musically correct and it showed a remarkable understanding of musical structure.

Genius

Wolfgang's ability on the clavichord and the violin was progressing at an incredible rate, and Nannerl was also developing into a fine musician. She did not, however, show Wolfgang's innate genius and oneness with music. By the age of five or six, he had surpassed her in technical ability, and more importantly, he had begun to compose more of his own music.

Encouraged by their progress, at the beginning of 1762, when Wolfgang was nearly six, Leopold decided that it was time to show off his two brilliant children to the music world.

"He [Mozart] is one of the most charming lads imaginable: there is a wit and feeling in everything he says and does, united with the grace and charm of his age. In fact, his liveliness relieves one of the fear that so premature a fruit might fall before it is ripe."
Mechior von Grimm, 1760s.

Wolfgang's mother, Anna Maria Mozart. Although Wolfgang's parents were often separated when Leopold embarked on lengthy tours with Wolfgang, there was a genuine love between them. Anna Maria doted on Wolfgang and allowed him considerable freedom when, near the end of her life, mother and son made a musical tour of Europe together.

Salzburg was a relatively small place and its people a little unadventurous in their attitudes. Leopold knew that it was no place to display his children's talents and began to organize a trip to the capital of Bavaria, Munich, where he hoped their skills would receive the recognition they deserved. It was to be the first tour of many for young Wolfgang, the childhood genius.

Munich

Every year the people of Munich held a carnival, or *Fasching*, which involved an endless whirl of concerts and balls. Leopold decided that this would provide a perfect opportunity to launch the children's career.

In the eighteenth century there were no public concerts in this part of Europe and most music was performed at the Royal Court or in the homes of the nobility. In order to break into this social circle, it was essential that a visiting musician could

produce letters of introduction. Further invitations would then come via word of mouth. Once the royal family showed an interest in the performer, doors were immediately opened to the homes of the rich and influential throughout the land.

So, in January 1762, with letters of introduction to the reigning Prince, Maximilian Joseph III, the Mozart family set out for Munich.

The Court of Maximilian Joseph was overwhelmed by the brilliance of the Mozart children and in particular with the great skill of the tiny Wolfgang whose father had given the impression his son was even younger than he was. As well as playing complex duets with his sister, Wolfgang played solo and even performed musical tricks, such as playing the clavichord with the keys covered by a piece of cloth.

The Mozart children became an overnight success in Munich and were the talk of high society. After their first performance they were invited to play night after night in a series of grand houses in

Above: During the Mozarts' first visit to Vienna in 1762, Wolfgang and his sister, Nannerl, were introduced to the Emperor Joseph I and the Empress Maria Theresa. Wolfgang was acclaimed as a child genius, a musical prodigy. He played set pieces and performed musical tricks that astounded the Royal Court.

Opposite: Wolfgang Amadeus Mozart, a small boy of only seven years old, is dressed in his finest costume for a court performance – a performance at which he will be the main attraction.

Wolfgang Amadeus Mozart, aged only seven, at the keyboard. He composed his First Symphony at the age of eight – a musical form that is usually only tackled by the most mature composers. This amazing talent makes his name "Amadeus" meaning "Beloved by God" particularly suitable.

the city, eventually staying for three weeks before returning to Salzburg.

Vienna

With this encouraging start behind them, Leopold immediately set about planning a more ambitious musical venture. He decided to arrange a trip to the capital of Austria, Vienna, where Empress Theresa and Emperor Francis I held court.

Leopold Mozart was firmly of the opinion that the skills of his children could make the family's fortune if things were properly managed and they received enough exposure. He worked the children hard, keeping them to a strict daily routine of study and practice.

In the eighteenth century, Vienna was an important musical city, proud of its musical tradition and home to many of the great composers of Europe.

At the time of the Mozarts' visit, both Joseph Haydn and Christoph Gluck lived there and made a comfortable living from their music. A large group of famous Italian composers worked in the city, and it could boast of one of the finest orchestras in Europe.

The Mozarts set out by boat for Vienna in September 1762, arriving on October 6. Using a letter of introduction, Leopold managed to secure a private concert in a house in the city. It was hugely successful and word spread so quickly that they were summoned to perform at the imperial summer residence, Schönbrunn Palace, within days.

Scepticism

Despite their scepticism over the claims of genius preceding the family, the Court was amazed at the skill of the children. Again, Wolfgang performed musical tricks, and the Emperor challenged him to play a difficult tune using just one finger – this he proceeded to do perfectly.

The itinerary in Vienna was exhausting. The Mozarts often had to gallop from one grand house to another, sometimes fitting in three concerts a day. Even at the age of six, Wolfgang hated performing in front of people who did not appreciate or understand music – people who gossiped and caught up with society's latest "news" while he played. This humiliating situation occurred all too often as the Mozart children became the latest craze in aristocratic circles – "the Wunderkinder".

It was not surprising, therefore, that with such a strenuous work load, Wolfgang fell sick. He was unable to leave his bed for two weeks and lost a great deal of weight. When he did finally recover, Leopold decided that it was time for them to return home.

On the road again

Almost immediately, Leopold began to organize the next move in his plan for his children's glittering careers – a Grand Tour of the major capitals of Europe.

As he steam-rollered ahead with his schedule he gave very little thought for the feelings of his children or indeed his wife, Anna Maria. Leopold Mozart was very domineering and made all the decisions for the family. Anne Maria looked after the children's well-being as best she could and kept quiet about her concerns for their safety on such arduous journeys.

Travel in the eighteenth century was tiring and often dangerous. There were very few properly constructed roads and those that did exist were in a permanent state of disrepair. Many areas were troubled by highwaymen and the going was slow, especially in bad weather. The main means of transport was the mail coach which carried paying passengers, squashed into small, cramped carriages, barely protected from the weather. Rain often blew in through badly-shuttered windows and the wind whistled through the carriage. In winter it was impossible to keep warm as the coach trundled through the snow and sleet with no form of heating.

To keep himself occupied during the long, boring journeys between cities, Wolfgang created a fantastic imaginary land, which he called Rucken

"He [Mozart] was of a fiery disposition; no object held his attention by more than a thread. I think that if he had not had the advantageously good education which he enjoyed he might have become the most wicked villain, so susceptible was he to every attraction, the goodness or badness of which he was not yet able to examine."

Johann Schachtner.

"The greatest wonder in all Germany.... Imagine, if you can, a girl of eleven years who plays the most difficult sonatas and concertos ... with almost incredible ease. That alone would be enough to astonish many people. But we are transported with utter amazement when we see a boy of six years sitting at a harpsichord, and hear him not only playing the same sonatas, trios and concertos ... but also hear him improvising from his head, for whole hours at a time."

An Augsburg newspaper, 1763.

Above: Eighteenth century travel conditions were appalling – the most popular form of public transport was the mail coach. They were cramped and freezing cold during the winter, and unbearably hot in the summer. Yet, despite these conditions, the Mozart family toured many countries in this way.
Right: The Mozart family performing together: Wolfgang at the keyboard, Leopold on the violin and Nannerl reading the sheet music.

("Back"). Rucken was a world where everything moved backward and names were spelt in reverse. Nannerl was drawn into the fantasy and the two of them drew maps of the various parts of the land and made up stories about the people who lived there. Rucken had its own laws, history and geography. In Wolfgang's imagination, he was King of his fictitious world and he could indulge his every fantasy there.

The Grand Tour

For the Grand Tour, Leopold decided to rent a private coach with a servant rather than to subject the children to such extreme discomfort. The tour began on June 9, 1763. Leopold had been granted extensive leave from his position as Vice-*Kapellmeister* by the Archbishop Schrattenbach and the whole family set off on the first stage of the journey.

On the first day of the trip, a back wheel broke and they had to stop at a small town named Wasserburg while it was repaired. Leopold knew that the town had a good organ at the local church and took Wolfgang along to see it. Although the organ had been invented hundreds of years earlier, in the mid-eighteenth century it was going through a process of development. Many organs had only keyboards, but this was changing with the addition of foot pedals which gave the player a greater range of textures in the sound the organ could make.

Leopold played the organ and demonstrated the use of the pedals to Wolfgang. Enthralled by the sound and the range of the instrument, Wolfgang then insisted that he be allowed to play as well. To the amazement of the clerics and organ master at the church, Wolfgang pushed the organ stall away and played the instrument standing up, operating the pedals and performing beautifully, as if he had been playing it for several months.

After this astounding interlude, the family resumed their journey. The Mozarts' fame had by this time spread far and wide and they were in demand to perform at the homes of the nobility as well as

Wolfgang was presented to Louis XV's wife, Madame Pompadour, at the Palace of Versailles outside Paris in December 1763. Leopold remembered her as a haughty woman, but the family were received very well by the French court.

Wolfgang performed before Parisian high society in early 1764. While the young Mozart played the harpsichord, the audience ate, drank and chatted among themselves. Even at the age of eight, Wolfgang disliked performing in front of people who did not appreciate or understand music or who did not listen intently.

at the courts of local rulers in each city they visited. It was the miraculous skills of the boy-prodigy who looked even younger than his seven years that everyone had to hear.

Paris

After their successes within the Holy Roman Empire, the Mozart family continued on to Paris – one of the biggest, most glamorous and wealthy cities in Europe. Leopold now believed that if the children were to be fully recognized for their brilliance anywhere it would be here.

At first, however, Leopold found it difficult to

break into Parisian society. Help came in the form
of a man named Baron Melchior von Grimm, a
leading intellectual figure among the aristocracy
there. He was tremendously impressed with
Wolfgang in particular and managed to secure
invitations for the children to play in the houses of
the French nobility. As usual, word of the Mozarts'
performance spread quickly. Just before Christmas,
they were invited to move to the Royal Court at
the Palace of Versailles where King Louis XV and
his family resided in a grandiose style.

Wolfgang and Nannerl delighted the royal family
with their performance on New Year's Day, and the
French nobility, famous for their haughtiness, were

surprised to see the warm affection the royals lavished on the Mozart family.

After their reception at Versailles, every door in Paris was opened to them and they began a series of performances in the city. Unfortunately, at this point Wolfgang again fell sick and was forced to stay in bed with a throat infection.

Despite Leopold's nervous fretting and fears that they would lose the momentum they had gathered with the local nobility, there was nothing he could do but to wait for his son to recover.

By March, Wolfgang was completely well again and he and Nannerl gave a hugely successful public performance. Unusually they made a lot of money from this, which greatly helped the finances for the tour. More often than not musicians were rewarded for their performances with gifts such as watches and snuff boxes. Beautiful and lavish as these gifts were, they usually had to be pawned to pay for rooms and food. Leopold was always resentful of the fact that even the immensely rich royal family could not find it in themselves to pay the musicians in cash rather than passing on unwanted trinkets they themselves had been given by visiting dignitaries or foreign ambassadors.

It was in Paris that Wolfgang's first compositions were published, four sonatas (K6, K7, K8, K9) for clavier with violin accompaniment.

A sonata is a lengthy piece of music usually composed for one or two instruments, and although these first attempts were relatively simplistic, they were quite exceptional.

In April they left Paris to travel to London.

Köchel numbering

Wolfgang Mozart, with his disorganized and spontaneous way of life, did not keep his compositions in any kind of order. Even in these early years he composed many pieces. In the nineteenth century, a botanist and Mozart-devotee, Ludwig Von Köchel, upon discovering the disorganized state of the composer's work, undertook the task of arranging Mozart's compositions into chronological order.

"No money, but a fine gold watch. At the moment ten carolins would suit me better than that watch which, including the chains and the mottoes, has been valued at twenty. What one needs on a journey is money; and let me tell you, I now have five watches. I am therefore seriously thinking of having an additional watch pocket on each leg of my trousers so that when I visit some great lord I shall wear both watches ... so that it will not occur to him to present me with another one."

Wolfgang Mozart, late 1770s.

Today, all Mozart compositions have an associated Köchel, or "K" number.

Another great admirer of Mozart was Albert Einstein. He revised the Köchel list in the 1930s. This system of numbering compositions is unique to Mozart – the K number of each piece is given in brackets after the piece is mentioned. Other composers use the term "opus", meaning "number" to identify their work.

London

The Mozarts eventually reached London on April 22, 1764. Within five days of their arrival, Wolfgang and Nannerl were performing before King George III and Queen Charlotte.

London was another of the great cultural cities of Europe. The arts were greatly appreciated and patronized by the royal family and the aristocracy. The composer Handel had been the preferred court composer until his death in 1759 – five years before the arrival of the Mozarts. The son of Johann Sebastian Bach, Johann Christian Bach, was the Queen's music teacher and an internationally-respected composer living in the city.

Wolfgang met Johann Christian Bach soon after arriving and the pair immediately struck up a warm and lasting friendship. On many occasions the thirty-year-old man and the eight-year-old boy played together on the newly-invented pianoforte performing duets. On one occasion, they played a solo by taking turns with a few bars each. According to one writer who witnessed the event, the music, quite incredibly, sounded as though it were being played by only one pianist.

The Mozarts performed frequently, several times before the King and Queen, and at an endless succession of aristocrats' houses. They also gave many public concerts where the children caused as great a sensation as they had in the cities of mainland Europe. They had a regular booking at a tavern called the Swan and Hoop in the City of London and Leopold even arranged for the public to come to listen to the children playing at home between

"The sensitivity and precision of young Mozart's ear are so great that false tones or those which are too sharp or too heavy cause tears to spring to his eyes. This still very young child is quite natural and utterly charming."

Dr. S.A.A. Tissot, from "Aristide", 1766.

This portrait of Mozart aged nine was painted when he was in London in 1764 and 1765. Not only did Wolfgang look younger than his years but his father, Leopold, publicized him as being a year younger. Many rivals believed it impossible for a child so young to be able to play and compose so well.

Wolfgang spent a large part of his childhood moving from city to city. The journeys were terribly uncomfortable and tedious for a young child. Wolfgang, locked in an adult world of musical performances, would make up games and faraway lands where he could be the ruler.

twelve and two o'clock each day.

Wolfgang gained greatly from his visit to England and grew enormously as a musician and composer during this time. He met many musicians and singers and composed a number of pieces, now realized as being very much influenced by J.C. Bach.

One of his most important compositions from this time was his first symphony in the key of E flat major (K16). A symphony is an extended piece of music which is divided into shorter sections called movements. In Mozart's time, the symphony was a relatively new musical form, but was greatly developed by Haydn and Mozart and taken even further by Ludwig van Beethoven after Mozart's death.

As well as his first symphony, Mozart wrote a collection of six sonatas for clavier and violin or flute, which he dedicated to Queen Charlotte.

Fake?

After a few months in London, a number of musicians began to grow jealous of the boy's great talent and word began to spread that Wolfgang was in fact much older than he was said to be. A scholar, Daines Barrington, decided to test him to determine whether it was true.

The musical tests were strenuous. Wolfgang had to rapidly compose music to express "love" and then "anger", as well as to undergo tests on his dexterity. Between tests Barrington studied the way Wolfgang behaved and noticed how immature he was about almost anything other than music. Barrington noted how Wolfgang enjoyed playing with a cat and that between tests he would make up games, such as pretending a broom was a horse and galloping around the room on it.

When it came to music however, Wolfgang played and composed like a highly-accomplished adult. Soon after his investigation, Barrington delivered a report of his findings to the Royal Society in London. The cynics and sceptics were silenced. Barrington believed Wolfgang to be a boy of eight or nine, but with quite exceptional musical talent beyond his years

Returning home

In July 1765, over a year after their arrival, Leopold decided to leave London. Wolfgang was most sad to leave his friend J.C. Bach, who continued to keep in touch with the Mozarts until his death nearly twenty years later. They were to return to Salzburg by a route through a number of European cities where performances could be arranged. On the return journey near disaster struck: both Wolfgang and Nannerl fell sick with intestinal typhoid. After many weeks, they both recovered. The family stayed on tour for several months before returning to Salzburg on November 30, 1766, three-and-a-half years after leaving.

The Grand Tour had been a tremendous success in both financial and musical terms and Wolfgang, not quite eleven years old, was now a world-famous

"Mozart is the greatest composer of all. Beethoven 'created' his music, but the music of Mozart is of such purity and beauty that one feels he merely 'found' it – that it has always existed as part of the inner beauty of the universe waiting to be revealed."

Albert Einstein.

Above: Wolfgang aged eleven. At this stage he had composed a number of sonatas and concertos. Below is the title page of his first published works – four sonatas for clavier and violin. Mozart's talent was different to the talents of other composers who struggled desperately to get their music down on paper – he wrote his neat copy, with only a few corrections, the first time.

musician. However, Leopold seems to have given little thought to the emotional and physical toll the tour had exerted on his family and most especially, Wolfgang. Such neglect inevitably played a role in the problems Wolfgang later faced as he tried to find his place in the world at large and to establish himself in a secure career.

Smallpox

Salzburg seemed very dull after spending so much time in Europe and the local nobility insisted on treating Wolfgang as though he was a freak of nature or a particularly able servant, rather than the internationally-famous musician and composer he had now become. After ten months in Salzburg, writing a vast amount of music, he was once more on the road, going with the family to Vienna.

There were two reasons for the trip. Firstly, Empress Maria Theresa's daughter, Maria Josepha, was about to marry and always with an eye for the main chance, Leopold realized that new music would be needed for the celebrations. Secondly, the one great musical form with which Wolfgang had never been given the opportunity to experiment was opera. He desperately wanted a commission to write an operatic piece and saw it as the ultimate form of musical expression. Opera was particularly popular in Italy, but was expensive to perform.

An opera is really a musical play where an extended piece of music, which can often be several hours long, is paired up with a story, where the singers take on acting roles. It begins with an instrumental piece called an overture. Usually, the best known pieces in an opera are the *arias* or "songs", where singers have the opportunity to show off their solo skills. These are punctuated by choral sections and recitatives, where the performers talk rather than sing a part. These breaks help to convey the story, or *libretto*.

Disaster

However, the Mozarts' trip was a disaster. Soon after their arrival, the royal bride-to-be caught smallpox and died. Vienna was thrown into a period of mourning and all festivities instantly stopped. Along with many others, the Mozarts fled the city, to avoid the disease.

But it was too late, both Wolfgang and Nannerl had become infected. Fortunately, they both survived, but for Wolfgang, death came very close and the world nearly lost a young man who would later develop into one of the greatest composers of all.

The first opera

By Wolfgang's twelfth birthday in January 1768, the family were once more back in Vienna. This time, with the recent tragedy over, the Emperor Joseph II, who always showed a great fondness for Wolfgang, invited the young composer to write an opera in Italian.

Wolfgang had yearned to write an opera ever since he had been introduced to the musical form during his first visit to Munich when he was only six years old. He planned to compose a piece called *La Finta Semplice*, (The Simple Pretence) and began work immediately.

However, all did not go well. The Viennese Court was plagued with intrigue and petty jealousies among the court musicians and composers. The musical scene there was dominated by Italians who resented the idea of a twelve-year-old, Austrian boy receiving a commission for an opera written in Italian. They tried to imply that he was not actually writing it himself and managed to persuade singers and musicians involved in the project to boycott rehearsals and to generally cause as much trouble as possible. Eventually these difficulties became too much and Mozart was forced to cancel the opera and return to Salzburg angry and bitterly disappointed. He had written over 550 pages of music and spent nearly six months working on it.

But all was not lost. "The Simple Pretence" was rescued by Leopold's patron, the Archbishop of Salzburg, and performed to great acclaim in the city a few months after their return, giving Wolfgang his first real taste of success in his home town.

"Virtually every piece he [Mozart] wrote, however hurriedly, is imbued with the elusive quality of greatness: moments which leave the audience profoundly and even physically stunned by their wisdom, tranquility, phenomenal beauty and effortless execution. At times he seems simultaneously to be breathing the most intimate secrets to the innermost soul of the individual, and to embrace the whole of humanity in vast and supremely logical statements."

Jane Glover, the conductor, from *Mozart: The Man, The Music and The Myth*, "The Sunday Times".

The Milan Opera House where "Mithridates, King of Pontus" was first performed on December 26, 1770, a few weeks before Wolfgang's fifteenth birthday. He had written this opera while touring Italy earlier in the year and returned to Milan for rehearsals. It was a huge success, with crowds of people cheering after each aria and giving standing ovations.

Italy

To be accepted as a musician of any note in Europe, a composer was expected to be a success in Italy, for it was here that many of the great musicians and composers of past centuries had been born or had made their mark. In December 1769, Leopold arranged a tour of Italy. Leopold was once again given leave of absence from the Archbishop, who saw Wolfgang as a great advertisement for the cultural excellence of his dominion.

On this occasion, Wolfgang and his father left Anna Maria and Nannerl in Salzburg.

They stopped in Milan, where Wolfgang created a stir with his evident musical talents. They arrived soon afer the Christmas carnival season had begun. Wolfgang was enchanted by the fact that the audience were in festive dress including traditional carnival masks of every description. Unlike his father, he was a natural extrovert and always enjoyed extravagant parties and carnivals.

Nonsense

During his travels, Wolfgang wrote letters to his mother and to Nannerl. His letters to his sister are full of nonsense and reminders of his imaginary land of Rucken, as well as bawdy jokes. Throughout his life, Mozart exhibited a lavatorial, often crude, sense of fun which he used to full effect. In one letter he describes a stage-character he had seen in an opera "who, whenever he jumped, let off a fart". He describes how ugly certain prima donnas were, on and off stage. Ever the perfectionist, he was often scathing about certain singers who always started their parts too early or too late.

Although they saw little of one another as adults, Wolfgang was very close to his sister throughout their childhood years, and his letters from Italy are often witty and affectionate. In one he wrote … "Have you heard what happened here? I shall tell you. We left Count Firmian's today to go home and when we reached our street, we opened the hall door and what do you think we did? Why, we went in. Farewell, my little lung. I kiss you, my liver,

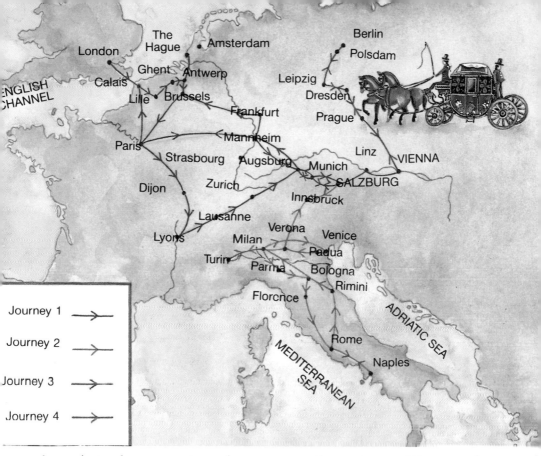

The map shows various European cities connected by journey routes, including:

Berlin, Polsdam, Amsterdam, The Hague, London, Leipzig, Ghent, Antwerp, Calais, Brussels, Dresden, Lille, Frankfurt, Prague, Paris, Mannheim, Linz, VIENNA, Strasbourg, Augsburg, Munich, SALZBURG, Dijon, Zurich, Innsbruck, Lausanne, Verona, Venice, Lyons, Milan, Turin, Padua, Parma, Bologna, Rimini, Florence, Rome, Naples

ENGLISH CHANNEL, ADRIATIC SEA, MEDITERRANEAN SEA

Journey 1 →
Journey 2 →
Journey 3 →
Journey 4 →

and remain as always, my stomach, your unworthy brother, Wolfgang."

Wolfgang was ecstatically received in Italy, and was even mobbed by the audience after his first public performance at the Accademia Filarmonica. The scenes which met him as he left were not unlike those the Beatles received during their heyday centuries later. Wolfgang was, most definitely, the greatest "pop-star" of his age.

A map of Europe tracing Mozart's many long journeys between 1763 and the late 1770s. In a world with no radios, records nor compact discs, it was mainly due to his regular visits to the cities of Europe that Mozart was able to build on his early reputation.

Opera

Milan was a city renowned for its critical appraisal of music. Thanks to an influential fan of Wolfgang's, Count Firmian, they were readily accepted into the houses of the rich and famous of the city. Once again the audience gave him a warm welcome and were amazed by his mastery of music. All cynicism disappeared when they heard him play.

Milan was famous throughout Europe for its opera and an invitation to write for the opera season there was seen as proof of acceptance by the musical establishment.

For Wolfgang the invitation came before he left the city. He was offered a contract to write the first opera in the following year's season and promised to return to compose it at the end of the summer. A dream come true.

Official acclaim

In Bologna, Wolfgang met the famous Padre Martini who was recognized as the greatest scholar of music in Europe. An endorsement of musical ability from the Padre gave any composer or musician a tremendous degree of prestige throughout Europe.

At their meeting Padre Martini set Wolfgang a series of rigorous tests, which the fourteen-year-old passed with ease. He left the city having performed a succession of highly-acclaimed concerts, as well as receiving the Padre's enthusiastic seal of approval.

While in Italy, Wolfgang spent some time with the great singer Manzuoli, whom he had first met and befriended in London. Shortly after, he met the English violin virtuoso, Thomas Linley, who was about the same age as Wolfgang. The two boys immediately struck up a great friendship which lasted until Linley's tragic death at the age of twenty-two.

In Rome, Wolfgang and Leopold attended a performance of the choral piece Miserere by the composer Allegri in the Sistine Chapel of the Vatican. When they returned to their rooms, Wolfgang wrote out the music from memory after only a single listening. When the authorities heard of this feat they were amazed because the music was sacred and it was forbidden to make copies of the score. By this single act alone, Wolfgang's unique musical talent had been vindicated beyond doubt. Rome joined the rest of Italy in unreserved admiration

"I had never before heard anyone play with such intelligence and grace. I was particularly overwhelmed by an adagio and by several of his extempore variations for which the Emperor chose the theme, and which we were required to vary alternately, accompanying one another."

Muzio Clementi, after a musical contest between himself and Mozart.

for Mozart's unparalleled genius.

On July 8, the Pope, Clement XIV, conferred on Wolfgang the Order of the Golden Spur. He was one of the youngest, at fourteen, to have received such an award and two days later, he was granted an audience with the Pope.

Wolfgang never took the knighthood very seriously. To Wolfgang such an award was of little importance and he never used it to further his career. He cultivated an anti-establishment attitude to rulers and nobility throughout Europe. Unfortunately for him, it was not within his nature to exploit his talent and the success he had achieved at a very early age.

In this way, Leopold and Wolfgang were at extreme ends of the spectrum. Leopold was forever pushy and ambitious for his son, whereas Wolfgang had a very relaxed and lighthearted approach to life which, although endearing, was to cause him considerable problems in later life.

Soon after becoming a Knight of the Golden Spur, Mozart was invited to take some musical tests at the Accademia Filarmonica in Mantua. Once again, he passed the tests with almost mocking ease and was immediately made an Honorary member of the Accademia.

"Mithridates, King of Pontus"

As they had promised, the Mozarts returned to Milan later in the year and Wolfgang began work on the commissioned opera, *Mitridate, Re di Ponto* (Mithridates, King of Pontus).

Once again, intrigues and rivalries hampered the rehearsals for the opera and both Leopold and Wolfgang had to struggle to prevent a repeat of the fiasco surrounding "The Simple Pretence" two years earlier.

The opera was finally performed on December 26, 1770 and was an immediate success. It ran for over twenty performances in Milan, where the audiences loudly applauded each *aria* and gave standing ovations at the end.

Because of this huge success Mozart was immediately given two further commissions, one to

"Mozart wrote everything with such ease and speed as might at first be taken for carelessness or haste; also he never went to the pianoforte while composing. His imagination held before him the whole work clear and lively once it was conceived. His great knowlege of composition made easy for him the general harmonic panorama. One seldom finds in his scores improved or erased passages."

From Niemetschek,
first biographer of Mozart.

Above: Another portrait with the Mozart family playing together. Although Nannerl had shown a great deal of talent musically, Leopold promoted Wolfgang as the young miracle.

Right: Count von Colloredo succeeded Archbishop Schrattenbach as ruler of Salzburg in 1771. Colloredo and Wolfgang became fierce enemies. Their relationship ended when Mozart could no longer stand Colloredo's total disrespect for his talents.

compose the music for the wedding of Maria Theresa's son, Ferdinand, which was to take place in Milan in October 1771 and the other, an opera for the new Carnival season.

Leopold and Wolfgang returned to Salzburg to write the pieces in March 1771. They had been away for fifteen months. Wolfgang's voice had broken and he had grown a little taller.

Wolfgang wrote throughout the summer and the two pieces were delivered in October 1771. Both projects were extremely well-received and encouraged by this success, Leopold approached the newly-married Archduke Ferdinand in an effort to secure his son a permanent post as court musician in Milan. He failed.

A death in Salzburg

Mozart stayed on in Milan for most of the Carnival, and arrived back in Salzburg on December 15. The very next day, Leopold's patient and considerate employer, Archbishop Schrattenbach, died.

This was to prove to be a significant turning point in the lives of the Mozart family. Leopold had spent seven of the previous nine years touring with his son. Schrattenbach's successor was Count von Colloredo, who was of an entirely different disposition to the former Archbishop.

At first, the new ruler demonstrated tolerance and patience with the Mozarts and their incessant travels and self-promotion. He even paid a very generous sum for one of Wolfgang's latest collection of pieces and immediately gave Leopold leave to accompany his son to Milan for the performance of his latest opera.

However, during the coming years, Colloredo's relationship with the Mozarts was gradually to deteriorate. Wolfgang had taken an instant dislike to him. He found the man extremely abrasive and overly proud of his lofty social position. Colloredo was arrogant and lacked charisma. He disliked old people or those in a weaker social or physical position to himself and had little understanding of music. He particularly disliked short people and so

"He [Mozart] would be moved to astonishment and perplexity if he could revisit and learn that he is safe with the greatest of those who have illumined and transfigured existence.... His attitude to his art was almost professional; he composed much as craftsmen making Chippendale. He described himself as 'soaked' in music; he composed habitually."
Sir Neville Cardus, from "Cardus on Music".

"Sometimes Mozart's inexhaustible gift to compose had inevitably to nourish itself on notes and ingenuity. The flawless execution happened as instinctively as the weaving of a bird's nest, which of course is one of the wonders of creation."
Sir Neville Cardus, from "Cardus on Music".

Wolfgang, being only above five feet in height, annoyed him even more.

Mozart had always resented being treated as a servant, which is exactly how Colloredo saw him. He began to hate his authoritarian employer; but for the moment at least, he was obliged to keep his temper and to play his role, dreaming of the day he could leave Salzburg and Colloredo's employ once and for all.

Court appointment

Thus began a less happy period of Mozart's life. For the next five years he spent most of his time composing in Salzburg. During this time he was becoming increasingly frustrated with Colloredo and the general lack of appreciation for his talents shown at the Salzburg Court.

For his part, Colloredo was growing increasingly angered by the Mozarts, seeing them as conceited little men with ideas above their station. But, because the rest of Europe seemed full of undinting praise for Wolfgang, he realized that having him in his employ served to highlight the cultural status of his court throughout Europe.

Colloredo appointed Wolfgang, aged sixteen, as leader of the court orchestra in August 1772, but the salary was far from impressive and it was considered a rather lowly position and far beneath Mozart's true value. Wolfgang accepted, however, and for a while at least managed to quell his tongue and to try to tolerate Colloredo's elitist and arrogant attitude.

Mozart still managed to travel as much as his employer would allow. He returned to Italy in October to attend the première in December of his new opera *Lucio Silla,* which was again a huge success at the Milan Carnival and ran for twenty-six performances.

Back in Salzburg by the spring, Mozart spent an intense period composing. During this time he wrote a collection of concertos, which usually highlight one particular instrument and are shorter than symphonies. Within a few years he had written five

violin concertos (K207, K211, K216, K218, K219), a piano concerto (K271), a symphony in G minor (K183) and an opera.

Whenever possible, Leopold managed to gain leave of absence for both himself and his son and the two of them made brief trips abroad to attend special concerts to play commissioned pieces, but always with the ulterior motive of trying to secure Wolfgang a prestigious position at a foreign court.

They met with little success, and meanwhile, when at home, Colloredo was becoming increasingly unfriendly. He did not in the least appreciate Wolfgang's obvious genius and even went as far as to say on one occasion, that the young Mozart knew nothing about music and should go to a conservatoire in Naples in order to learn!

Colloredo dismissed Wolfgang but kept Leopold in his employ.

Wolfgang decided that it was time he left the city to try his luck elsewhere. Apprehensive of his son's

The Austrian city of Salzburg is situated at the edge of the Austrian Alps. In Mozart's time it was a relatively small city compared to Paris or Vienna and Wolfgang was eager to travel and enjoy life to the full elsewhere. Today the city is full of Mozart memorabilia even though Mozart was never fully appreciated here during his lifetime.

safety, and knowing him to be terribly irresponsible with money and careless about who he chose for friends, Leopold insisted that Wolfgang's mother go with him.

More travels

After a tearful farewell, Wolfgang and Anna Maria set off in September 1777, leaving Leopold to look after Nannerl and to continue his duties at court.

The intention was for Wolfgang and his mother to head for Paris, where it was hoped that Wolfgang could secure an important post and make a good living.

Mozart was now nearly twenty-two and had changed a great deal in recent years. Although he still adored his parents, he was gaining a greater sense of independence from the intensity with which Leopold had run his life. Away from the watchful eye of his father and accompanied only by his doting mother, Wolfgang began to let his hair down.

During his travels through Europe he took to staying out late, attending parties and social gatherings with an ever-growing group of friends, while his lonely mother, homesick for Salzburg and her husband, stayed at their lodgings.

Mozart did little composing at the time, but managed to earn some money from teaching. He wrote long, reassuring letters to his father, but when, through Anna Maria, Leopold learned of his son's antics he was far from pleased.

Aloysia

Things finally came to a head when news reached Salzburg that Wolfgang had met and fallen in love with a singer by the name of Aloysia Weber.

The Webers were a poor family. Aloysia had three sisters and a brother. Frau Weber was a strong and determined woman and her husband was a music copyist with few prospects. Leopold Mozart suspected that the Webers saw Wolfgang as a great prospect for the future and that they wanted to marry off their daughter.

A scene from the 1984 film "Amadeus" showing Mozart (seated) at a party imitating other composers' styles. Mozart was a very complex character combining an eccentric sense of the ridiculous with serious emotions. He was always the extrovert who loved socializing and playing the fool. Yet his music is perhaps the most serene and perfect ever composed. He exercised the childish side of his personality by buffoonery and expressed his deeper side in the great music he wrote.

Wolfgang had eccentric ideas of launching Aloysia onto the Italian opera scene as a great new talent. Leopold decided the idea was foolish and wrote scathing letters to stop his son and make him leave immediately for Paris.

A return to Paris

Wolfgang was eventually persuaded and set off for Paris in March 1778. The trip was a disaster from the start. Whereas he had been received there with adulation as a child prodigy fifteen years earlier, Paris was a very different proposition for a twenty-two-year-old composer – for all his brilliance.

His one contact was the old family friend, Baron Melchior von Grimm. Von Grimm tried his best to help Wolfgang, but breaking into Parisian society was an uphill struggle.

Mozart and his mother had to stay in cheap accommodation and hardly managed to spare enough money to buy food. After paying for carriages to and from performances there was nothing left. To Mozart's intense annoyance, the nobility who invited him to play in their homes insisted on paying with useless gifts rather than in cash.

With the exception of a symphony in D major, known as the "Paris Symphony" (K297), Mozart composed little during his stay. The Paris Symphony was perhaps his greatest composition up to that time and is seen today as an early masterpiece still frequently performed around the world.

Meanwhile, as Mozart tried in vain to establish himself, by April, his mother, Anna Maria, had fallen sick. With a poor diet and an insanitary water supply, as well as living in cheap damp rooms, she grew steadily weaker. Wolfgang was worried for her and both he and Anna Maria wrote pathetic letters to Leopold describing the miserable lives they were leading in Paris.

Over the next few months her condition grew worse and she became delirious. The doctor could do little for her and she died in July 1778.

Mozart was devastated and could not bring himself to tell his father the dreadful news by letter.

"He is too sincere, not active enough, too susceptible to illusions, too little aware of the means of achieving success. Here, [Paris] in order to succeed, one must be artful, enterprising and bold; for the sake of his fortunes, I could wish [Wolfgang] had half as much talent and twice as much of the qualities I have described.... You may see, my dear Sir, that in a country where all the mediocre and detestable musicians have made immense fortunes, your son could not manage at all."

Baron Friedrich Melchoir Grimm, in a letter to Leopold Mozart, 1778.

Instead he called upon the help of a family friend, Abbé Bullinger, to do the job for him.

Heartbroken, he left Paris almost immediately and set off for Salzburg via a long route which would take him to Munich where the Webers now lived. His intention was to visit Aloysia and to propose marriage.

Disputes

Things had changed while Mozart was in Paris. When he met Aloysia she had become a successful singer, a *prima donna,* and no longer showed any interest in the struggling young composer. Thwarted in love, Mozart returned to his family in Salzburg.

To earn a living, he once again turned to teaching, something he always hated. His loathing for the need to teach middle-aged, unmusical, but wealthy people had never left him and he hated even more the need to flatter and pay lip-service to what he saw as stupid nobility. Worse still, he was forced to go back to his old position as orchestra leader for Colloredo.

Wolfgang began to argue with his father and resented him interfering in his private life. Leopold treated him as a child and was forever trying to temper his son's over-spending and natural waywardness. For his part, Wolfgang was still as reckless with his finances as he had ever been. All he wanted was to compose all day and to socialize each night.

"Happiness and sorrow play like sunlight and shadow through Mozart's music, swiftly, innocently. A happy turn of melody comes, and we are made happy, too. Then, as suddenly, pathos surprises us, steals out of the serene air, and – here is the crowning pathos – not only overcomes us but, surely, Mozart himself."

Sir Neville Cardus, from "Cardus on Music".

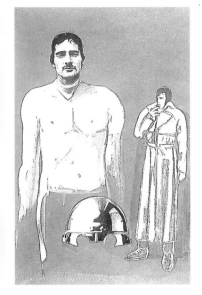

A modern day poster for a performance of Mozart's opera "Idomeneo", to be performed in Berlin. Mozart's operas have been re-interpreted in many different ways in the past two hundred years and some performances have moved a long way from the original theatrical story, but have kept the unforgettable music.

"Idomeneo"

At last, late in 1780, some relief came in the form of a commission to write an opera for the Munich Festival of 1781.

In November 1780, Mozart was given six weeks leave by Colloredo. He set off immediately with the music for the new opera already half arranged in his mind. The opera was named *Idomeneo,* and it was an instant success. Mozart suddenly found himself the focus of musical attention in Munich.

When his leave expired, against Colloredo's instructions, Mozart decided not to return to Salzburg and he stayed in Munich hoping to secure new commissions on the strength of his immensely popular opera.

However, this latest bid for freedom failed again. Archbishop Colloredo was visiting Vienna and ordered his orchestra leader to join him there.

When Mozart arrived Colloredo insisted that Mozart should eat with the other servants and be at his beck and call to perform music Colloredo wanted, when he wanted it.

Mozart did his best to control his fiery temper but eventually declared that he was resigning.

Although penniless and unemployed, Mozart was free at last. Against his son's wishes, Leopold tried his best to persuade Colloredo to accept him back, but this time things had gone too far. Mozart would never work for the man again.

Freedom

Mozart threw himself into the hectic Viennese social scene and gradually began to establish a life for himself there. During his first few months in the city he wrote six violin sonatas, and managed to pay his rent by again returning to teaching.

In July 1781, he was asked to write an opera in Vienna with a libretto in German – an ambition he had been nurturing for a long time. He chose a controversial story about a Turkish harem called "The Abduction from the Seraglio" and began work on it immediately.

Meanwhile, the Weber family had moved to

Vienna after the death of Herr Weber. Mozart had remained in touch and paid frequent visits to their house. Soon he had taken up lodgings there.

Mozart was happy in Vienna at this time. Frau Weber and her daughters looked after him well and he had plenty of time to work on the new opera. He was earning enough money to live and had a large circle of friends in the city.

However, Leopold was displeased. He saw Frau Weber as manipulative and did not approve of Wolfgang's interest in another of her daughters, eighteen-year-old Constanze.

The younger Mozart saw things differently. Constanze was not pretty, but displayed a genuine affection for him and he enjoyed her company. According to some stories Frau Weber was so desperate to see Constanze married that she spread gossip that Mozart had treated her daughter badly, thereby practically forcing the couple to the aisle.

Leopold was furious and tried his best to persuade his son to return to Salzburg. Mozart refused. By the end of 1781, his new opera was finished and he was full of optimism for the future. As he approached his twenty-sixth birthday, Mozart decided it was time he settled away from home permanently and that he could make a success of things in Vienna.

He proposed to Constanze in December 1781 and she accepted. They set the date for their wedding for the summer of the following year.

Marriage

The couple were married on August 4, 1782 in St. Stephen's Cathedral in Vienna. It was a happy occasion despite Leopold's resistance. A wedding feast was laid on by a wealthy friend, Baroness von Waldstadten, and the couple were invited to dinner by the famous composer, Gluck.

The day after the wedding, Wolfgang and Constanze received Leopold's consent by letter, although he still expressed concern at his son's "waywardness".

"The Seraglio" was first performed a few weeks before the wedding and was another huge success

Wolfgang's vivacious and loving wife, Constanze Mozart. They made a good pair: disorganized, untidy and full of fun. They lived, with their two sons, in constant confusion and near poverty which only seemed to help Mozart in his work.

Above: A scene from Mozart's operatic masterpiece, "Don Giovanni". Mozart dealt with many important issues in his music and often introduced new musical tastes to the audiences. Sometimes they were a success and sometimes they were not. This opera was a critical and popular success throughout Europe, but did little to help Mozart's finances.

Right: A scene from "The Abduction of the Seraglio" that was performed in Vienna shortly after Constanze and Wolfgang were married.

both in Vienna and in other cities. Mozart's fame as an opera composer of worth was beginning to spread throughout Europe. In March 1783, a Hamburg music magazine claimed that the thirteen-year-old Beethoven could one day develop into a composer as great as Mozart if he continued to progress at his present rate.

This was perhaps Mozart's most successful period although there was still precious little financial reward for his achievements.

Wolfgang and Constanze Mozart lived in a number of cheap rented apartments in Vienna. He taught a great deal and almost secured the post of music master to the Princess of Württemberg, but was finally beaten by a far lesser musician, Georg Summer.

Jealousy

Many composers in Vienna were jealous of Mozart. The large contingent of Italian composers at court were particularly venomous. Of this group, Antonio Salieri was Mozart's worst enemy. It is likely that Salieri and his friends were instrumental in Mozart's continual failure to secure a worthwhile position at court.

He taught most mornings, visiting his pupils in their homes, and composed during the afternoons and evenings. During this period he wrote three piano concertos in the keys of F, A and C (K413, K414, K415), which are now regarded as examples of his finest work. He also began a mass in C minor (K427).

Nights were spent in a constant round of parties. Being immensely talented and always willing to entertain, Mozart was a popular guest, was a natural extrovert and loved to drink and dance.

Constanze was devoted and kind-hearted, and the couple shared a playful, happy-go-lucky approach to life. However, like Wolfgang, she was not very practical with money and did not manage the household very well. During the nine years they were married she bore six children, but only two survived infancy.

Antonio Salieri (1750-1825) was a well-known and respected composer in his day although his music is very rarely performed today. Salieri was far more successful than Mozart in securing influential and well-paid employment. The role Salieri played in Mozart's decline and eventual death has been greatly exaggerated, but it is true to say that he did hinder Mozart's career through jealousy.

The first child

The Mozarts were leading a life-style which they could ill afford and they were slipping further into debt. Leopold could do little but watch his son make what he saw as a mess of his life.

The Mozarts' first child, a boy named Raimund, was born in June 1783 and strange as it may seem, they left the baby with foster parents and went to Salzburg to see Leopold. The visit went well and Leopold finally accepted the partnership. However, upon their return to Vienna, the couple found that their baby had died.

Mozart overcame his grief by throwing himself into his work. He had been commissioned to perform a series of evening concerts throughout the winter months, but was so busy with teaching and composing other pieces that he often had to write the music for the concerts immediately before the evening's performance. On a number of occasions, he had nothing prepared but a hastily written lead part and had to improvise, or make up, his accompaniment on the spot.

Freemason

In 1784 Mozart joined a Freemasons' lodge, Beneficence Lodge. Freemasons are a brotherhood of individuals dedicated to helping one another, a form of secret society with their own strict rules and code of conduct. Mozart relied heavily on his masonic friends during the late 1780s, borrowing heavily from others in the brotherhood, often having to humiliate himself by writing begging letters in order to secure loans he knew he could probably never pay back. Freemasonry was frowned upon by many at court and it served to polarize his position, drawing on the help of others in the brotherhood but further alienating his enemies who were not part of the order.

In the spring of 1784, Mozart, aged twenty-eight, fell gravely sick with what is now thought to have been a serious kidney infection. It was the worst illness he had so far suffered and caused him a great deal of pain. Many historians think that it was in

Wolfgang Mozart became a Freemason in 1784. The Freemasons are a secret society whose roots trace back to the twelfth century. Here an initiation ceremony is taking place with all the special rites involved. In some ways, Mozart's membership was of great use as he received considerable financial help from his fellow Masons but, being an illegal organization, it also made him many enemies in high places.

fact this disease which was the main reason for his early death, seven years later.

It took until the summer for him to recover fully and things were further complicated by the fact that Constanze was pregnant throughout the illness. She gave birth to their second child in the summer, a boy who survived. They named him Karl.

Meanwhile, Wolfgang's sister, Nannerl, had married and Leopold, who was now in his mid-sixties, was left alone in Salzburg. Wolfgang invited him to stay with them in Vienna, and he arrived in February 1785.

Chaos

Wolfgang proudly introduced his father to his many friends, including the famous singer Michael Kelly and one of his closest companions, the great composer Joseph Haydn. Haydn had tremendous respect and admiration for Mozart's work, and the two of them often performed concerts together in the Austrian capital.

Wolfgang tried to make his father's stay in Vienna as exciting as possible and along with Constanze, led him into the whirl of night life in the city. The Mozart household was as chaotic as their social lives. There was a continuous stream of visitors at all hours of the day and night. They lived in a cramped apartment among the noise and mess created by bringing up a small baby. To add to this there was the smell of a collection of family pets – a dog, Guckel, and a bird, Starl, whose song is reputed to have influenced a number of Mozart compositions.

Amid the confusion, Mozart still managed to compose. In fact, this was one of his most productive periods. He seemed to thrive on chaos, as long as he could lock himself away in relative peace to pour out his music.

Leopold could now see that his son was successful – even if he was not rich. Wolfgang was in great demand and one highly-acclaimed composition followed another.

However, by April 1785, Leopold's patron back

"Madame Mozart told me, that great as his genius was, he loved dancing. He was a remarkably small man, very thin and pale, with a profusion of fine fair hair, of which he was rather vain. He always received me with kindness and hospitality.... He gave Sunday concerts, at which I was never missing. He was kind hearted and always ready to oblige, but so very particular when he played, that if the slightest noise were made he instantly left off."

Michael Kelly, the singer, and Mozart's friend.

in Salzburg, Colloredo, was threatening to terminate his salary if he did not return immediately.

As father and son said their farewells, neither could have known that it would be the last time they were to meet.

"The Marriage of Figaro"

Soon after Leopold's return to Salzburg, Mozart was commissioned by Emperor Joseph II to write another opera. For his subject he chose a highly controversial French play called *Le Mariage de Figaro,* by the writer, Beaumarchais. Although it was very popular in France, Joseph II had banned the play from the Viennese stage earlier that year.

On the surface, the story line was innocent enough, a simple tale of a tangled love affair that revolved around a young man who becomes a valet to an aristocrat in order to make a living.

"All the original performers had the advantage of the instruction of the composer, who transfused into their minds his inspired meaning. I shall never forget his little animated countenance, when lighted up with the glowing rays of genius – it is as impossible to describe it as it would be to paint sunbeams."

Michael Kelly, the singer, describing the rehearsals for the première of "The Marriage of Figaro".

VERITABLE EXTRAIT DE VIANDE LIEBIG.

LES NOCES DE FIGARO, Opéra de Mozart. Nº 2

Left: "The Marriage of Figaro" is now considered to be the most perfect opera ever to have been composed. At the time of its performance in Prague everyone went Figaro-mad, singing catchy tunes all over the city. Inset: The opera is so popular and well-known today that it is even used in advertising campaigns.

However, the politics underlying the plot were considered to be dangerously subversive. The aristocrat and his family are made to look foolish and the valet, Figaro, finally solves everyone's problems and emerges as the hero of the piece. Figaro himself is a political radical who believes that a man should be judged by his achievements and not by the social position of his parents.

The music for this opera was alien to that first audience in the 1780s. They had not heard anything so violent, shocking and so intellectual. Mozart was making powerful statements on a wide range of topics which had never been done before.

Fortunately, Mozart had teamed up with a first-class librettist, Lorenzo da Ponte, who was the official stage poet in Vienna. His understanding of the interaction between the libretto and the music was a perfect complement to Mozart's beautiful, complex melodies and harmonies. But, above all,

Lorenzo da Ponte was the librettist for three of Mozart's most accomplished operas – "The Marriage of Figaro", "Don Giovanni" and "Cosi Fan Tutte". He was a well-respected poet in Vienna and enjoyed a close working relationship with Mozart spanning almost four years.

"Here they talk about nothing but 'Figaro'. Nothing is played, sung or whistled but 'Figaro'. No opera is drawing like 'Figaro'. Nothing, nothing but 'Figaro'. Certainly a great pleasure for me!"

Mozart, in a letter from Prague, January 1787.

between them they managed to tone down the political aspects of the original story so as not to offend the Emperor and yet preserve the essence of the tale.

The rehearsals were plagued by the intrigues of jealous rivals. Salieri was particularly defensive because he wanted his own newly-completed opera to be performed before Mozart's.

In a rage, Mozart threatened to put his score on the fire unless his opera was performed first. When the Emperor heard of this he intervened and sided with Mozart. Salieri had to wait.

"The Marriage of Figaro" was first performed on May 1, 1786 at the *Burgtheater* in Vienna. Mozart was extremely nervous at the première, but despite a number of technical problems, it was received with delight and was hailed as a great success. At last, Mozart was achieving the recognition he deserved.

Financially, the opera was of little importance. He was paid little more than the usual payment for a concert and yet the amount of effort involved in completing such a masterpiece was incomparable. To make more money, Mozart had to keep writing music for his regular concerts in the city – on top of his teaching responsibilities and other lesser commissions. Even so, he still had to resort to borrowing from the other members of his Masonic lodge.

Despite the huge success of "Figaro", performances of operas by other composers rapidly followed and the fickle Viennese soon forgot about it. Only abroad, particularly in Bohemia, was the full magnificence and brilliance of Mozart's achievement realized. To the people of Prague especially, the thirty-year-old composer was the greatest of them all, and it was to Prague that Mozart turned for his next commission.

"Don Giovanni"

Mozart received the commission for *Don Giovanni* in February 1787 and its première in Prague was set for October of that year. He knew he would have to work fast and began immediately.

Once again he collaborated with da Ponte who

adapted an Italian play, "Don Giovanni Tenorio", for the libretto. "Don Giovanni" is a moral tale based on the story of Don Juan, a wandering scoundrel, who spends his time seducing women and charming his way through life, never doing a day's work and caring for no one but himself.

In the opera, Don Juan becomes Don Giovanni. He has a man-servant, the comical Leporello, who does everything for his master, from acting as look-out for jealous husbands to finding the next meal. After a series of adventures and near-death fights at the hands of angry ex-lovers, Don Giovanni finally gets his just treatment at the hands of a giant stone statue which comes to life and casts the villain into hell.

Partnership

The story-line gave both da Ponte and Mozart huge scope for intense drama. There are several crowd scenes in the opera which provided Mozart with great opportunities to compose grand pieces for many voices in which to show off his unparalleled harmonic genius. The scene where the statue of a commandant whom Don Giovanni had murdered appears and confronts Don Giovanni is probably one of the most dramatic scenes ever written into an opera.

As a team, Mozart and da Ponte were to create some of the most moving operas, but the demands of the new commission became too much and infection he had first suffered three years earlier. For a time he had to stop work altogether.

To make things worse, he heard in March that his father, Leopold, was gravely ill. During recent years, father and son had drifted apart as Wolfgang had carved out his own life and set up home with his own family in Vienna, but there remained a deep-rooted love between them. Wolfgang was too ill to visit his ailing father, but was reassured that his sister, Nannerl, was looking after him.

Leopold died on May 28, 1787. When Wolfgang heard the news he was naturally devastated. He was too weak to attend the funeral and grieved with his wife and child in Vienna.

The character, Leporello, from Mozart's opera "Don Giovanni". Leporello was Don Giovanni's servant who acted as accomplice to his master's raucous schemes. Here he is holding the list of his master's many female "conquests".

Above: Street musicians performing Mozart's music in Prague, the city that perhaps appreciated the composer's work during his lifetime beyond all others. Mozart's music is not confined to the houses of the nobility nor the concert halls today – it is played all over the world in a variety of settings.
Right: "Don Giovanni" being performed today – the operas are constantly performed internationally to great acclaim.

Not surprisingly, Mozart was unable to finish *Don Giovanni* in time for the planned first night of October 14 and the première was postponed until October 29.

Mozart threw himself into the task of completing the work, but by the night before the dress rehearsal he had still not written the overture.

Thinking that her husband would certainly have completed the opera by then, Constanze had organized a party. To the amazement of his friends, Wolfgang enjoyed the party, giving no thought to the imminent première for which the music was still unfinished.

Finally, after a long night of heavy drinking and revelry, Constanze dragged her husband to a quiet room where he began to write the overture, kept awake by her conversation and a large jug of punch. By the morning the music was finished.

The next evening *Don Giovanni* opened to an ecstatic reception. Against all the odds, Mozart was once again the toast of Prague.

An appointment in Vienna

Realizing that he could not possibly better his success in Bohemia, Mozart returned to Vienna.

In his absence, the composer Gluck had died. He had held the post of court composer and at his passing the position was open to a successor.

The large contingent of Italian composers in the city, Mozart's rivals, were all vying for the prestigious appointment. Although he had not the slightest doubt about his suitability, Mozart did not believe that he would be given the appointment because of the influence of the others at court.

However, he was wrong. At the age of thirty-one, he achieved his ambition of an official appointment at a European court, an achievement which would have made Leopold proud.

The starting salary for the post was half of that received by Gluck and was barely enough to sustain the family. However, Mozart was allowed to teach independently and it gave him official endorsement to devote his time to his first love – composition.

"The music of 'Don Giovanni' was the first to make a deep impression on me. It awoke a spiritual ecstasy which was afterwards to bear fruit. With its help I penetrated into that world of artistic beauty where only great genius abides. It is due to Mozart that I have devoted my life to music. He gave me the impulse to all my efforts, and made me love it above all else in the world."

Peter Ilych Tchaikovsky.

"But it wasn't intended to go down easy. Mozart himself was deeply committed to a wide range of social issues.... In 'Don Giovanni' you don't have all of the cast members come to the front of the stage ... and sing, at the top of their lungs, in a C major military march 'Viva la libertà!' two years before the French Revolution – thirteen times, which is how often they sing it – if you don't actually intend to push your public."

Peter Sellars, from "A World of Ideas".

Above: Vienna, an important cultural city and home to a large community of composers, poets and painters during the time that Mozart lived there.
Opposite: Inside Mozart's house – it was at this desk that he wrote many of his greatest concertos and the score for "The Marriage of Figaro".
Inset: A scene from the film "Amadeus" showing Mozart furiously trying to finish a score late into the night, while Constanze sleeps – a routine the Mozarts often followed.
Below: The Villa Bertramka in Prague, the house they shared during the 1780s.

Don Giovanni opened in Vienna soon after his appointment but was not well received. The Viennese were very conservative in their musical taste. *Don Giovanni* was an innovation in its day and placed serious demands on the attention of the listener.

Fortunately, the Emperor was full of praise for the work, but was reported to have said, "That opera is divine. I should even venture that it's more beautiful than *Figaro*. But such music is not meant for the teeth of the Viennese." In response to which Mozart was reputed to have whispered, "Give them time to devour it!"

Because of the Emperor's enthusiasm and the high praise the opera received from Mozart's friends in the city, *Don Giovanni* was performed a number of times. Eventually even the Viennese began to appreciate it.

Mozart was gaining a foothold in Vienna as a composer of note, but the problems of how to make ends meet were becoming even more acute.

Poverty

Mozart's success in Vienna was short-lived and by early in 1788, he was again forced to borrow heavily from his Masonic contacts.

In the summer, the family moved to a house a little way outside the city. For Mozart's creativity it was a good move. Within the space of six weeks he wrote three of his greatest symphonies, Nos 39, 40 and 41 (K543, K550, K551), for a new series of concerts to be held in the city.

This amazing feat is seen by many historians as Mozart's greatest achievement. All three symphonies were written at the peak of his musical creativity and are considered as masterpieces, frequently performed throughout the world to this day. The last symphony, No 41, was nicknamed the Jupiter symphony in the nineteenth century and is perhaps his best.

Domestically, however, the move to the country was a mistake. Pupils could not travel out for lessons and Wolfgang missed the energy of the city.

Then disaster befell the couple when their youngest child died at the age of six months.

Wolfgang somehow managed to smother his grief by working to the point of exhaustion, but for Constanze it was a traumatic experience. By the end of the summer they had returned to Vienna and moved into a small apartment.

Mozart wrote little during the winter of 1788-9. At the same time his concerts had become less popular, and audiences had declined. The music he was commissioned to write in his role as court composer was often trivial. He found the job frustrating and the results did little for his reputation. It was a bleak time for the family.

Finally, in the spring of 1789, hope arrived when a friend of Mozart's, Prince Karl Lichnowsky, asked if the composer would accompany him on a business trip to Berlin. Mozart jumped at the chance.

"I only wish I could impress on every friend of mine, and on great men in particular, the same depth of musical sympathy and profound appreciation of Mozart's inimitable music that I myself feel and enjoy; then nations would vie with each other to possess such a jewel within their frontiers.... It enrages me to think that the unparalleled Mozart is not yet engaged by some imperial or royal court! Forgive my excitement, but I love the man so dearly!"

Franz Joseph Haydn.

Berlin

The trip served as a welcome break from the depression of Vienna, but Mozart was homesick. He wrote home almost every day, relating various incidents that happened.

Breaking the journey in Leipzig, Mozart played the organ in St. Thomas' Church on which the great composer, Johann Sebastian Bach, had first performed his famous pieces. He spent hours studying Bach's original scores. "Now here is something one can learn from!" he declared.

From Leipzig they moved on to Berlin, where Mozart turned up unannounced at a performance of his opera, "The Seraglio". For a while, he sat quietly at the back of the auditorium, but after only a few bars he realized that the orchestra was not terribly competent. Exasperated by the playing, Mozart found himself edging further to the front of the auditorium. When the second violin played a D sharp instead of a D, he shouted out "Damn it all! Will you play a D!" Word rapidly spread through the shocked audience that the eccentric little man at the front was in fact Mozart himself....

Although Mozart enjoyed the trip it did little for his career. He received a commission to compose six string quartets and six piano sonatas for the Berlin court, but it did not bring him the thing he most wanted – an appointment worthy of his genius.

Soon after his return, Constanze fell seriously ill and he was again forced to borrow money to pay for her expensive medicines. It was decided that she should make the journey to the health spas at Baden and that, in her absence, Karl should be sent to a boarding school.

Suddenly, Mozart was alone in Vienna for the summer. He felt uninspired and unhappy having to compose simple dance pieces and incidental music for the court, with little but continued hope that his situation would soon change for the better.

> *"Dearest little wife, if only I had a letter from you. If I was to tell you all the things I do with your dear portrait, it would make you laugh. For instance, when I take it out of its case, I say 'Hello Stanzerl! Hello little scamp, kitten-face, little button nose, little trifle, Schluck-und-Druck....' O Stru! Stri! I kiss you 1095060437082 times and am your most faithful husband and friend, Wolfgang!"*
>
> Wolfgang's letter to his wife, in 1789.

"Cosi fan tutte"

The end of the year brought mixed fortunes. Constanze, still ill, had fallen pregnant and after a difficult pregnancy gave birth to a girl in November while at the spa. The baby died soon after birth.

One positive thing to happen that year was a commission from Emperor Joseph II to write another opera. Mozart renewed his partnership with Lorenzo da Ponte and threw himself into an intense period of composing.

The opera opened at the *Burgtheater* in Vienna in January 1790 and was again a success.

Cosi fan tutte is a comedy focussed around two young army officers, Ferrando and Guglielmo, who have a wager with an elderly acquaintance, Don Alfonso, that their fiancées will be faithful to them while they are away fighting. To test their fidelity, the soldiers visit the girls in disguise only to discover that they manage to win them over. To complicate

"Cosi Fan Tutte" which Mozart wrote during 1790. It was the last opera for which da Ponte wrote the libretto and is a light-hearted piece exploring the themes of love and jealousy.

"I like an aria to fit a singer as perfectly as a well-tailored suit of clothes."

Mozart, in a letter to his father, February 28, 1778.

---

matters, the two sisters fall in love with each other's fiancé.

At first the soldiers are outraged at their own success and are only saved from a jealous scene with the women by Don Alfonso who had instigated the wager in the first place. In the end all is forgiven and the original couples reconcile.

The success of *Cosi fan tutte* was unfortunately short-lived. A month after its première, Emperor Joseph II died and court mourning ended all entertainment until the summer.

To compound the problem, da Ponte, who had the approval of the late Emperor, had to leave Vienna in a hurry because of his enemies at court. Thus ended one of the most fruitful partnerships in the history of music. Mozart and da Ponte had together created three of the greatest operas so far composed and the ending of their relationship was a great loss to the world of music.

Desperation

In the summer of 1790 Constanze once again returned to Baden. In Vienna the new Emperor, Leopold II, made radical changes at court and Mozart failed to secure the position of Vice *Kapellmeister* and was lucky to retain his post as court composer.

Because his salary was still barely sufficient to pay for the family's accommodation, Mozart returned to teaching, which he found even more frustrating than he had in previous years of hardship.

In September 1790, the King and Queen of Naples visited Vienna for the double wedding of their daughters. Salieri and others of the musical establishment were commissioned to write celebratory music – but Mozart was cruelly ignored.

In October, the Emperor was crowned in Frankfurt. Mozart was not invited to attend the coronation with the other musicians from Vienna. So, he pawned his silver to rent a carriage to get there.

Even this desperate move failed. He did not receive a single commission and performed his piano concerto in D major (K537), now known as the "Coronation", to a sparse audience.

Depressed and exhausted he returned to Vienna.

"The Magic Flute"

Early in 1791, a fellow Mason and old friend of Mozart's, Emanuel Schikaneder, had invited him to write an opera to be performed at the *Theater auf der Weiden* where Schikaneder worked as an impresario and actor. The *Theater auf der Wieden* was a far simpler venue than the Royal Court. It was like the nineteenth century music hall.

The libretto for the opera, *Die Zauberflöte*

Emanuel Schikaneder, an actor and theatrical entrepreneur who commissioned Mozart to write the music for "The Magic Flute", his last opera. Schikaneder was a Mason and wrote the libretto which was full of Masonic imagery. He also appeared in the first performances of the opera in Vienna, 1791.

A portrait of Wolfgang Amadeus Mozart in his early thirties, painted one hundred years after his death. It is rather a flattering portrayal of a man who, near the end of his life, suffered recurring bouts of a severe kidney complaint that had plagued him for years. It also expresses an uncharacteristic seriousness that Wolfgang himself might have thought rather formal.

("The Magic Flute"), was written by Schikaneder himself and was a fairy story full of masonic imagery. It is full of references to giant snakes and magical quests (Masonic symbols), and has been thought by many to be rather infantile. This criticism however, could never be levelled at the music.

Mozart was very sick throughout this period. He kept himself going by taking a series of exotic medicines and smothering the pain by drinking and working ridiculously long hours.

Constanze was away in Baden for much of the summer and in July, she gave birth to a boy they named Franz. This second child went on to become a musician who lived until 1844.

After months of intense work, Mozart finished writing the final notes of "The Magic Flute" the night before its première on September 30, 1791.

He was unwell at the first performance, but insisted on conducting the orchestra himself. Nervous about its reception, he was overjoyed and relieved by the thunderous applause at the end.

"The Magic Flute" was performed over twenty times in October alone and the enthusiasm of the audience increased nightly. Even Mozart's old enemy at court, Salieri, attended the opera and was vocal in his praise for the music.

Once again there was a chink of light in the darkness of Mozart's life. If he was not to be acclaimed by the establishment, then at least there was an audience for his music.

The mysterious visitor

In July 1791, when Mozart was working on "The Magic Flute", a tall stranger visited Mozart and left him an anonymous letter requesting that he compose a Requiem Mass. The stranger was persistent and returned a number of times to hurry along the commission. Mozart was deeply disturbed by the visits and soon found himself obsessed with its composition when he was meant to be working on "The Magic Flute".

He became convinced that he was writing the Requiem for himself and was frantic with worry and stress. One theory put forward is that the dark stranger had been hired by Mozart's rival, Salieri, to visit Mozart and pay him in gold pieces to compose a Requiem Mass.

Indeed, Salieri and Mozart were enemies for most of Mozart's time in Vienna. But, by the end of Mozart's life, it is truer to say that the two composers enjoyed a less frosty relationship. There is no doubting that Salieri always had a great respect for Mozart's work, but was too proud and jealous to actively help the struggling musician.

However, the Requiem was actually commissioned by a rich, but untalented, amateur composer named Count Franz Walsegg-Stuppach as a tribute to his own wife. The Count's intention was to pass off the composition as his own, hence the secrecy. However, as events transpired, this plan backfired when Constanze found the unfinished manuscript after her husband's death and exposed the fraud.

The final weeks

By November 1791, exhausted from months of trying to compose both a Requiem Mass and "The Magic Flute", Mozart was sick again with a recurrence of his kidney infection.

The family's financial situation, which had always been precarious, was worsening daily. There now seemed little hope of the composer ever establishing himself in a salaried position which could keep them in a life-style his abilities deserved and his tastes demanded.

Wolfgang tried to work on the Requiem, but progress was slow. Constanze returned to Vienna in October to find her husband weak and depressed. During a walk one day, he burst into tears and told her that he thought he had been poisoned.

In his semi-feverish condition, Mozart was quite certain that the Requiem was his own epitaph, and grew increasingly anxious about finishing it.

Suffering blinding headaches and an increasing paranoia that he was writing the music for his own funeral, Mozart collapsed on November 20 and was forced to bed. His hands and feet had become swollen and he went through long spells of vomiting as a result of the kidney infection.

"[Of 'The Magic Flute'] The opera ... is the only one in existence that might conceivably have been composed by God."

Neville Cardus, from "The Manchester Guardian", 1961.

Over page: An orchestra performing Mozart at the Philharmonic Concert Hall in Berlin, Germany. Today, Mozart's music is performed world-wide and is among the best loved and most popular classical music performed. During the 1991 bicentenary of Mozart's death the world's major concert halls performed the full list of his work and special festivals were organized to celebrate the work of one of the greatest composers who ever lived.

Now running a very high fever, Mozart was seriously ill. But, between long periods of sleep or incoherence he still insisted on continuing his work on the Requiem Mass.

In early December, realizing that the end was near and with the Requiem still unfinished, he gave strict instuctions to his pupil, Süssmayr, as to how to complete the work if he were to die.

In the first few days of December, Mozart's fever worsened and periods of consciousness and lucidity became less frequent. Finally, on December 5, 1791, Wolfgang Amadeus Mozart, aged thirty-five, died.

His last act was to try to make the sound of drums in his Requiem for his assistant to record in the score.

Funeral

In death as in life, Mozart did not receive the recognition due him. He should, in a just world, have had a funeral worthy of his talent, a ceremony such

Above and below: The finest musicians are trained on Mozart's music. It is some of the most beautiful music ever composed and yet Mozart was given a pauper's funeral and, today, no one knows where he is buried.

as those reserved for heads of state.

However, in the Vienna of the 1790s, all but the aristocracy were buried in municipal graves; Emperor Leopold II was opposed to elaborate funerals. So, being neither noble nor a statesperson, this great composer was buried in an unmarked pauper's grave with a small group of mourners made up of friends and family following the coffin to the cemetery.

No one saw the actual burial, save the grave-digger who scattered quick-lime over the body after dumping it in an open grave occupied by five others.

To this day, nobody knows where Mozart's body was finally laid to rest. In eighteenth century Vienna, women were forbidden to attend funeral processions, and so even Mozart's beloved wife, Constanze, could not be with him.

Tribute

Today Mozart is seen as perhaps the greatest musical talent who ever lived. His music is now enjoyed by more people than ever before. Barely a day passes when his music is not performed at a concert hall somewhere in the world.

During his short lifetime, Mozart composed over forty symphonies, nearly twenty operas and operettas, over twenty piano concertos and twenty-seven string quartets, as well as a vast collection of sonatas, religious and incidental music.

For Mozart, composition appears to have been effortless, as natural as breathing, and we can only sit and wonder what beautiful music he may have written if he had not died so young.

Mozart was a man of extraordinary talent, a man who took a childlike joy in life. Combined with an abrasive attitude to authority, his one failing, his total inability to manage his own affairs, cost him dearly. Despite the exaggerated stories which have grown around the "Mozart myth", there is no doubt that his music, beloved by generation after generation, will last as long as there are people alive who appreciate its sublime beauty and unmatched perfection.

"Mozart's influence transcends history. Each generation sees something different in his work.... Mozart's music, which to so many of his contemporaries still seemed to have the brittleness of clay, has long since been transformed into gold gleaming in the light, though it has taken on the different luster of each new generation...."

Alfred Einstein, from "Mozart: His Character, His Work".

Important Dates

1756   Jan 27: Wolfgang Amadeus Mozart is born in Salzburg, Austria.

1761   At five years old Mozart composes his first pieces.

1762   Jan: Mozart gives his first performance before the Elector of Bavaria in the capital of Bavaria, Munich. He is only six years old.
Oct: Mozart first performs before the Emperor and Empress in Vienna, Austria.

1763   June: The Mozart family sets off on its Grand Tour of Europe.

1764   March: Mozart's first sonatas are published. He is eight years old.
April: The Mozarts arrive in London where they stay for fifteen months. Wolfgang meets J.C. Bach.

1765   July: The family begins the return journey to Salzburg. Wolfgang and Nannerl contract intestinal typhoid.

1766   Nov: The Mozart family arrives back in Salzburg.

1767   Sept: The family leaves for an unsuccessful trip to Vienna. Wolfgang and his sister Nannerl catch smallpox.

1768   Mozart's first opera, *La Finta Semplice*, is completed.

1769   Mozart, aged thirteen, is made third Concert-master to the Salzburg Court Chapel.

1770   Leopold and Mozart set off on the first Italian tour. Mozart writes his first string quartet.
June: Mozart, aged only fourteen, is made a "Knight of the Golden Spur".
Dec: *Mitridate, Re di Ponto* is performed to great acclaim in Milan.

1771   Dec: Wolfgang and Leopold return from the Italian tour. Archbishop Schrattenbach dies in Salzburg and is succeeded by Count von Colloredo.

1772   Aug: Mozart is appointed as leader of the Court Orchestra.
Dec: *Lucio Silla* is performed in Milan.

1773-77 Mozart spends a long period, largely in Salzburg, composing. A growing enmity between Mozart and Colloredo develops.

1777   Sept: Wolfgang, now twenty-one, leaves with his mother to embark on a new tour of Europe.

1778   Jan: Mozart meets Aloysia Weber in Mannheim.
March: Mozart arrives in Paris with his mother.
He composes the "Paris Symphony".
July: Mozart's mother, Anna Maria, dies in Paris.
Rejected by Aloysia Weber, Mozart returns to his father and sister in Salzburg.

1779   Mozart obtains the post as Court Organist at Salzburg.

1780   He is commissioned to write the opera *Idomeneo* for the Munich Carnival.

1781   After a series of rows, Mozart finally leaves Colloredo's service and settles in Vienna. He becomes increasingly interested in Aloysia Weber's sister, Constanze, and takes lodgings in the Weber home.
Dec: Mozart proposes to Constanze.

1782	July: *The Abduction from the Seraglio* is performed in Vienna. Aug 4: Wolfgang Mozart, aged twenty-six, marries Constanze Weber at St. Stephen's Cathedral, Vienna.
1783	The Mozarts' first child is born. The couple travel to Salzburg to visit Mozart's father, Leopold, and his sister, Nannerl. Upon their return to Vienna, they discover that their baby has died.
1784	Mozart falls seriously ill with a kidney infection. He becomes a Freemason. Constanze gives birth to a son, Karl. Mozart composes six piano concertos.
1785	Leopold Mozart visits his son in Vienna. Now twenty-nine, Mozart is at the peak of his success in Vienna and is composing at a very fast rate.
1786	May: *The Marriage of Figaro* is first performed in Vienna. Dec: *The Marriage of Figaro* is performed to huge acclaim in Prague.
1787	May: Leopold Mozart dies in Salzburg. Wolfgang, who is seriously ill, is unable to attend his father's funeral. Oct: Mozart's opera, *Don Giovanni,* has its première in Prague. He is appointed as successor to Gluck in the post of Court Composer.
1788	Mozart composes his last three symphonies, Nos. 39, 40 and 41, in the space of six weeks. He writes a series of letters to a fellow Mason, Michael Puchberg, asking to borrow money.
1789	Mozart visits a number of European cities with Prince Karl Lichnowsky.
1790	Jan: *Cosi fan tutte* is first performed in Vienna. Oct: Mozart embarks on a trip to Frankfurt for the coronation of Emperor Leopold II which fails to secure him any commissions.
1791	Mozart unsuccessfully attempts to secure the post of *Kapellmeister* at St. Stephen's Cathedral, Vienna. July: The Mozarts' second son, Franz, is born. Mozart is mysteriously commissioned to write a Requiem Mass by an anonymous stranger. He becomes convinced that he is writing for his own funeral. Sept 30: The first performance of *The Magic Flute* receives thunderous applause. Dec 5: Wolfgang Amadeus Mozart, aged thirty-five, dies in Vienna.
1991	The bicentenary of Mozart's death shows him to be the most popular classical composer in the world.

Musical terms

Aria: In *opera*, originally a song for one or more voices, but now for a *solo* voice.

Concerto: A piece of music using *solo* instruments and *orchestra*. Although some *concertos* feature more than one *solo* instrument, it is more usual to highlight a performance on a single instrument. A *concerto* is generally in three *movements*. Mozart is considered to have been the best composer in this musical form.

Duet: A piece of music written for two instruments.

Forte: A musical term meaning loud.

Harmony: The simultaneous sounding of notes in a way that is musically significant. A two-part *harmony* would consist of two series of notes played together, the notes forming a "harmonious" blend.

Improvise: To compose music without any previous preparation.

Key: A classification of the notes of a scale. Keys can be either major or minor. The key of C major is the simplest key in which to play. It involves the use of only natural notes i.e. no sharps or flats.

Libretto: The words of an opera, written by a librettist. The modern equivalent would be "lyrics".

Mass: The Catholic church service, in Latin, set to music.

Melody: A succession of notes varying in pitch and forming a recognizable musical shape. The technical term for "tune".

Movement: A part of a larger piece of music such as a *symphony* or *concerto*.

Musical score: Music written out on manuscript paper. The score contains all the parts to be played by the various instruments.

Opera: A musical play in which an extended piece of music is paired up with a story *(libretto)* and the singers take on acting roles.

Orchestra: Interpretation has changed over many years – the modern definition dates from the eighteenth century when the standard form was musicians playing together on four groups of instruments: stringed, wind, brass and percussion. The nineteenth century saw an increase in the number and varieties of instruments and the twentieth century a return to smaller groups.

Piano: A musical term for soft, a soft sound.

Requiem: A musical setting for the Mass of the Dead, which is in Latin.

Solo: A piece of music that is performed by one person, either alone or with other performers merely providing an accompaniment.

Sonata: A piece, often similar in length to a *concerto*, but usually only employing one or two instruments rather than an *orchestra*.

Symphony: An extended piece of music using a large scale *orchestra*. Usually in four *movements*, with the first and last quick, the second slow and the third a graceful dance-like piece.

Recommended listening:

Clarinet Concerto in A (K622)

Piano Concertos No 20 in D Minor (K466), No 21 in C (K467), No 25 in C (K503), No 27 in B flat major (K595)

The Requiem Mass (K626)

Operas: The Magic Flute, The Marriage of Figaro, Cosi fan Tutte, Don Giovanni

Eine Kleine Nacht Musik (Serenade for strings No 13 in G) (K525)

Symphony No 39 in E flat major (K543), No 40 in G minor (K550), No 41 in C major or "Jupiter" (K551)

Horn Concerto No 1 in D (K412)

Index